101 ~~~~~~~ Pocket Money

**Written by Rosy Border
Illustrated by Peter Wilks**

HENDERSON
PUBLISHING PLC

©1993 HENDERSON PUBLISHING PLC

THINK IT THROUGH

Most young people receive pocket money every week. A few have plenty of money left at the end of the week. Many, sad to say, have plenty of week left at the end of the money. Are you one of those? Then this book is for you!

You will find many suggestions - a hundred and one, to be precise - for earning extra money. Now nobody is going to find all one hundred and one ideas either appealing or possible. There won't be much demand for garden shed tidying in the city centre, for example. But every one of these ideas has been tried and tested by children between the ages of 8 and 13. It worked for them, and it could work for you. If you are skillful at something, you can use your skills to earn money. But another useful thing to remember is that some jobs are so mindlessly boring or downright messy that people will gladly pay for someone else to do them. That someone could be YOU. You might even enjoy the jobs other people hate so much.

ADVERTISE YOUR SERVICES

Word of mouth - "Tom cleaned my car/walked my dog last week and did a splendid job" - is a good way to get started. You do some work for a neighbour, who tells his friends, who tell their friends all about it.

This is fine, provided you know enough people to guarantee you plenty of work. But advertising reaches a wider audience.

In the days before home computers and desk top publishing, children with entrepreneurial ambitions - that is, an aim to go into business for themselves - used to give themselves writer's cramp, lettering notices and posters by hand. You may still have to do this. Many children, however, now have access to a computer whose printer will churn out copies at the touch of a button. Lucky kids. They can produce notices which they can push through letter boxes. They can produce posters and ask local shops to display them.

I know a bright lad who paid for a monthly ad in the village magazine. It didn't cost much, and it produced lots of customers. Of course, you will want to tailor your own advertising to suit your own needs. Do get permission before you do this. After all, Mum or Dad may end up taking some of your calls from prospective customers.

Is Your Garden Getting You Down?

Let us sort it out. Flower beds weeded and tidied.
Lawns mown and edged.
Greenhouses tidied.
Paths weeded.

Moderate rates.
Call David Jones
on 0728 831179.

You'll be glad you did!

Advertise where likely customers will see your ads. To advertise car cleaning, you might leave notices carefully tucked behind car windscreen wipers, or put up a poster at the local petrol station. Even better, make friends with a car park attendant and ask permission to put a notice behind the windscreen wiper of each car, offering your services while the owner of the car is out shopping. Offer ironing services on a poster at the local launderette. Dog walkers might put posters in a pet shop or a veterinary surgery, and so on.

RUNNING THE SHOW

Enterprising, hard-working people with plenty of contacts are often able to act as job centres for other people. One enterprising schoolgirl ran a babysitting agency, putting parents and sitters in touch with each other and taking 20 per cent of the proceeds. She made sure the sitters were properly paid, and that they were taken home afterwards. She made sure the parents got a fair deal too. So I have made **Running an Agency** number one on our list.

Two Words of Advice
If someone refuses your services, do not get angry. Remember, nobody HAS to employ you. Keep smiling. The person who turned you down may tell a friend, who WILL give you a job.

Secondly, remember that NOT everyone is kind and friendly. REMEMBER what you have been taught about strangers. If possible, work in pairs or groups. ALWAYS let your family know where you are going and when you hope to return. And NEVER get into a car with anyone you don't know.

1. Running an Agency.

Gather a group of friends together and write down their details: names, addresses and telephone numbers, skills on offer. You will probably want to keep a file or card index, with an entry for each worker and one for each customer. Suppose you want to offer a car cleaning service. You advertise it, and when people come forward, you put customers and car cleaners together. The customers pay you, and you pass the money on to your team, keeping a share - 20% is fair - for your trouble. In return for that 20% you have found work for your team, paid them their wages and made sure they did a good job.

ON THE ROAD

There are millions of cars on the road, and every one is a potential earner for you. But do remember: always ASK PERMISSION before touching anyone's property. Some people may not welcome your value-for-money service.

2. Cleaning Cars
Whether you head a clean-up squad or go it alone, you will need equipment. Luckily, most can be borrowed from home.

> **You need:**
> A bucket • a sponge • a hosepipe (if available) and a tap to connect it to • a soft brush to clean the wheels • a bottle of car shampoo (washing up liquid does the paint work no good at all) • some car polish or wax • a polishing cloth • a sponge to clean the windows and windscreens • a chamois leather

The best way to learn how to clean a car is to watch someone who is good at it. You will see them sponging or hosing the bodywork, drying it off with a "shammy". When you are sure you can do the same, you are ready to offer your services.

Although many car cleaners do a fine job alone, many work in teams like a production line in a factory. 'A' swabs the paint work, 'B' leathers off, 'C' cleans the glass, and so on.

3. Cleaning Windscreens

This is quicker than full scale car cleaning, and you don't need so much equipment. A bucket and a sponge should be enough. A friendly car park attendant will probably let you pounce on motorists when they arrive. Be slick, cheap and cheerful - but NEVER be a nuisance. A smile and a "Have a safe journey" will brighten your customer's day.

4. De-Icing

In cold weather, cars left outside are often covered with frost. With care, you can clear windscreens with a scraper (try a plastic kitchen spatula) in no time.

5. Mucking Out Cars

Most family cars are mobile dustbins, pleading for someone to clear out the used tissues, sweet papers, old receipts, etc.

> **You need:**
> A dustpan and brush or car vacuum cleaner
> A plastic bag for the rubbish
> Another plastic bag for "lost and found" items
> Window-cleaning spray
> Cloths to clean windows and trim (check with the customer before touching leather and wood trims in smart cars)
> Air freshener

Start by clearing out everything that isn't actually stuck down and putting each item into one of your bags. Don't forget the glove compartment and those little pockets on the doors. Then clean the seats, remembering the little crevices using a car vacuum cleaner or a dustpan and stiff brush. Clean the carpets - some can be removed and thoroughly beaten outside. Clean and polish the dashboard, etc. Clean the inside windows, taking special care with the windscreen. Finally spray air freshener to make the car smell as clean as it looks.

101 WAYS POCKET MONEY

6. Checking Tyres for Damage

Tyres pick up all sorts of things: flints, nails, even thorns. Any of these foreign bodies can cause a puncture. You can offer a tyre checking service. No special equipment is needed: just old clothes (you can get very dirty around cars), an old screwdriver and a piece of chalk. Check each tyre and with the screwdriver, carefully clear out any foreign bodies from between the treads. If you come across anything dodgy, such as a scuffed place or a tear in the rubber, mark it with your chalk or felt tip and tell the car owner.

7. Checking Tyre Treads

Tyre tread standards vary slightly from country to country, so you will need to check this. Bald tyres - tyres whose treads have worn down - are illegal and their owner can be fined. This is where you come in. Checking tyres takes all of five minutes. All you need is a tread gauge and a note pad. You measure the treads of all five tyres (remember the spare tyre!) and write them down. You tell the car owner the results of your examination, and claim your money.

NEVER crouch under a car or work in the road. Keep safe.

8. Cleaning Bicycles
You could combine this with servicing. See below.

9. Servicing Bicycles
Many families have several bikes but nobody to take care of them. You can check bicycle tyres, blow up any soft ones, mend punctures, etc. Test the chain; oil it if necessary. Check the brakes and adjust them if necessary. You could then attach a sticker with "This bike serviced by - " and your name and phone number.

10. Cycle Classes
Sensible, responsible children who have already passed cycle proficiency tests can earn pocket money by teaching little ones how to handle their bikes safely. Choose somewhere safe and put the tinies through their paces. You could give each "graduate" a home made certificate of success.

11. Be a Despatch Rider
Sometimes a bike is faster than a car for urgent messages!

RUNNING AROUND

For hundreds of years, young people have earned money by running errands. "Pop down to the shop for me, and fetch a loaf of bread" can be turned into a thriving business.

12. A Shopping Service

Make it known that you are available to do shopping. You must be businesslike about this.

> **You need:**
> a note pad and pencil
> a stapler
> a shopping bag or, even better, a trolley (if you are on foot)
> a bike with a SAFE carrier (no balancing goods on the handlebars, please).
> a purse for the money

If you are well organised, you can shop for several people at the same time. This is where the note pad comes in. Start a new page for each customer. Write the customer's name, the amount of money they gave you and a list of the things they want you to buy.

Always keep till receipts, write the name of the customer on each receipt and staple it to the list. That way you are unlikely to give the wrong change.

Many people are very glad to have a service of this kind. You can also keep an eye on old or disabled customers: if someone doesn't answer the door, this may mean that he or she is ill or hurt. Tell a grown-up at once.
There is more to this job than just earning money: you are helping people too.

13. Posting Letters and Parcels
Busy people will often pay for this. At Christmas, however, you can set up in opposition to the Post Office. Here's how:

14. Running Your Own Postal Service
Offer to deliver Christmas cards within, say, a one-mile radius for half the amount the Post Office charges. Many Scout troops do this to help their funds. You and your friends could do the same. You're unlikely to put the Post Office out of business.

15. Delivering Magazines
There's money in delivering newsletters, magazines, etc. You can also spot potential customers for other services as you do your rounds.

16. Parking Shopping Trolleys

If you visit a car park near a supermarket, you will see lots of people wheeling shopping trolleys to their cars. They load the loot and then face a trek back to the trolley park with the empty trolley. You can save them the trouble and earn yourself some pocket money too. Watch for likely customers. Offer politely to return the trolley.

Some supermarkets have special trolleys which cannot be wheeled away until someone puts a coin in a slot. With such trolleys, you can retrieve the deposit and take it back to your customer, who will probably want to give you a share for your trouble.

17. Retrieving "Lost" Trolleys

Supermarkets lose thousands of trolleys every week. They are expensive to replace and staff have to go out looking for them instead of working in the store. Make friends with the manager of your local supermarket and agree a fee for every lost trolley returned.

14   101 WAYS POCKET MONEY

18. Loading Shopping

It's amazing how many people have no idea how to load shopping into their cars. They put fresh-baked loaves under bottles of pop and wonder why their bread gets squashed. Learn how to pack a car boot and then offer your services. Remember the golden rule: heavy at the bottom, light at the top.

Remember also that bottles roll around when the car is moving, unless you pack things between them. Put frozen foods together to keep each other cool. And protect fruit from bruising: no one wants battered bananas or punctured pears.

LOADS OF RUBBISH

19. Emptying Waste Paper Baskets and Rubbish Bins

Busy people will often pay to have their bins emptied and the refuse sacks, wheelie bins or whatever put out for the dustmen. All you need is a pair of rubber gloves and a plastic refuse sack. Find out which day is rubbish day in which street, and offer a weekly service.

20. Recycling Waste Paper

One man's trash is another man's treasure, and you may know of local organisations which collect waste paper to sell to raise money for charity. Otherwise organise collections of waste paper to be taken to the nearest recycling centre. Paper is amazingly heavy, so a wheelbarrow or trolley is a great help here.

BEWARE OF BROKEN GLASS AND SHARP METAL!

21. Taking Bottles and Jars to the Glass Bank
You could charge so much per bottle/jar. They are heavy: use a wheelbarrow or trolley.

22. Taking Cans to the Can Bank
As above. Aluminium drinks cans are worth more than steel ones and many charities are glad to have them.

23. Taking Rubbish to a Skip
When someone has done some decorating or heavy gardening, they often hire a skip to take away the rubbish. If someone has space in their skip, you can ask their permission to go and collect rubbish from other people (who, of course, pay you) and put it in their skip.

HOMES AND GARDENS

There are lots of household tasks that people will pay you to do, provided you do a good job. The muckiest and most boring jobs are the ones most likely to be passed on to you! Here are just a few of them:

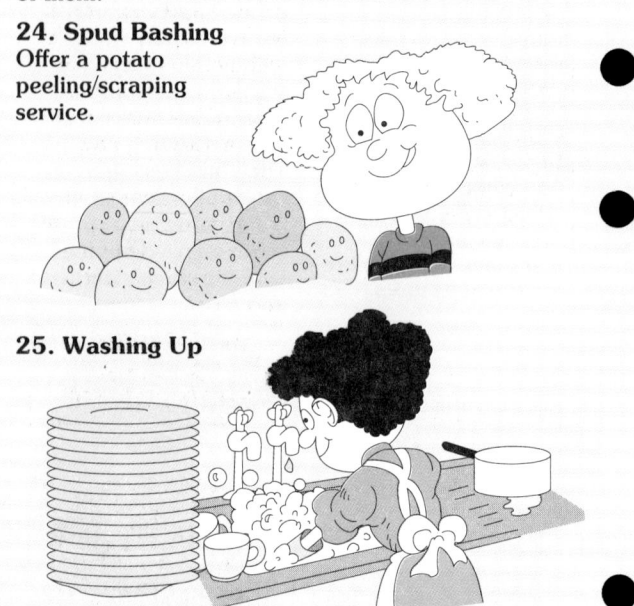

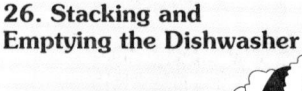

24. Spud Bashing
Offer a potato peeling/scraping service.

25. Washing Up

26. Stacking and Emptying the Dishwasher

27. Cleaning out the Oven

This is most housewives' Number One Hate, but it could be a nice little earner for you.

You need:
Rubber gloves
A can of oven cleaner
Cloths or sponges
Scouring pad
A bowl of soapy water
Newspapers to protect the floor and other surfaces

Follow the instructions on the can of oven cleaner, but you will probably have to heat the oven SLIGHTLY, spray the cleaner around and wait for it to act. While you are waiting, you can clean the oven shelves in a bowl of hot soapy water with a scouring pad. Then you can (hopefully) sponge all the accumulated gunge from the inside of the oven, leaving it fresh and clean.

WEAR RUBBER GLOVES THROUGHOUT.

A much cleaner job is:

28. Cleaning out the Fridge
No fridge ever gets as mucky as an oven!

101 WAYS POCKET MONEY

29. Doing the Fireplaces

You need:
Newspaper
Kindling or fire lighter
Matches
Coal or logs

Open fires make a mess, and someone may give you the job of clearing out the ashes and laying and lighting the fire. Remove the ashpan and dispose of the ashes. (NEVER put hot ashes in a dustbin). Then sweep the gate and fire surround. Make a bed of crumpled newspaper, lay kindling or pieces of fire lighter on top, then the coal or logs. The secret is to leave plenty of space for air to circulate. Fire cannot burn without oxygen, as your science teacher would tell you. Keep matches well out of reach of younger children. Do not light the fire yourself - this must ALWAYS be done by an adult.

30. Gathering Winter Fu-oo-el
(as Good King Wenceslas would say) Fill log baskets and coal scuttles and keep them full. Quite a task!

31. Cleaning Silver
(or brass, stainless steel, etc.)

You need:
A newspaper to protect the table
metal polish (one for brass, one for silver, etc.)
A cloth for applying the polish
A cloth for rubbing off the polish
A bowl of warm water to wash the silver afterwards
A tea towel

Follow the instructions on the polish can. In general, you apply the polish, let it dry a little, then rub it off, polishing as you do so. Then you wash the item and dry it. You could take along a personal stereo and have music while you polish!

32. Dusting Ornaments
Your aunt or granny may have whole menageries of china animals. A small job is to dust them and the surfaces they stand on. Even few pence a week for this would soon add up.

33. Cleaning out Cupboards
Many people will gladly pay someone to empty their kitchen cupboards, clean the shelves and replace everything tidily.

34. Clearing Up After a Party
People are often glad of someone to dispose of the rubbish, bring in stray plates and glasses and generally clear away after a party. Left-over snacks are a bonus!

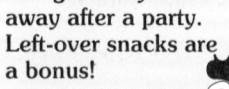

35. Hanging out Washing
(and bringing it in again BEFORE it starts to rain!)

36. Ironing
Some young people learn this at an early age, and a very useful skill it is. Many people hate ironing and will pay to have it done.

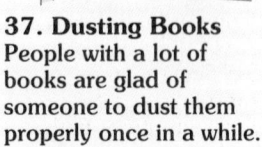

37. Dusting Books
People with a lot of books are glad of someone to dust them properly once in a while.

> **You need:**
> A soft duster
> An old shaving brush (or similar)

Dust the outside and, holding the book closed, brush the top edge, never attempt to remove dust from the tops of books by banging the books together. Do not attempt to hurry this work; hands must be washed frequently to avoid transferring dust from one book to another. If you cannot take this job seriously, stick to cleaning ovens.

OUTDOOR JOBS

38. Weeding Paths and Drives

Digging out the weeds from tarmac or gravel is boring, which is why many people will happily pay you to do it. It is, however, very easy, and "greener" than using weed killer.

> **You need:**
> A bucket
> A trowel or old knife
> Something to kneel on

Get down on your knees, dig out each weed and put it in the bucket.

39. Digging out Daisies

(and thistles and clover) from lawns requires similar equipment but is easier on the knees.

40. Weeding Flower Beds

This is trickier - unless you are skilled in weed recognition you really need lessons from someone who knows a dandelion from a prize chrysanthemum. Once you know, it's easy. Equipment as above, plus gardening gloves for prickly customers.

41. Mowing Grass
You need to know what you're doing: power mowers can be dangerous. "Push" mowers and shears are hard work, but less likely to cut off your toes.

42. Edging Lawns
Steer clear of power strimmers. These can be dangerous and heavy. You can get a very neat finish with shears.

43. Tidying Sheds
There is nothing hard about this, but few people seem to get around to it - which is where YOU come in!

44. Sweeping Patios
Ditto!

45. Clearing out Garages
And you could earn extra by taking rubbish away after both jobs (see above).

46. Tidying Greenhouses
As above; you can also...

47. Wash flower pots
Dirty flower pots spread plant diseases. Shake out the dry earth onto a newspaper, then wash each pot in a bucket of soapy water.

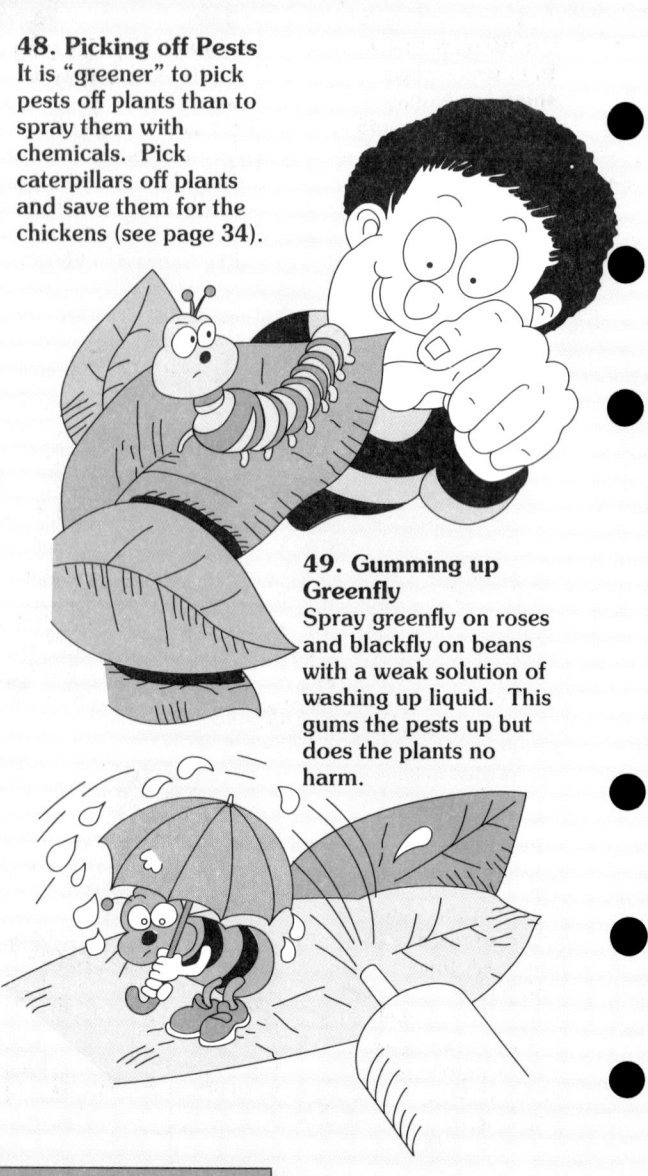

48. Picking off Pests
It is "greener" to pick pests off plants than to spray them with chemicals. Pick caterpillars off plants and save them for the chickens (see page 34).

49. Gumming up Greenfly
Spray greenfly on roses and blackfly on beans with a weak solution of washing up liquid. This gums the pests up but does the plants no harm.

50. Watering Gardens
In times of water shortage, when everyone is forbidden to use hosepipes and sprinklers, many gardeners are grateful for someone to go round with a watering can.

51. Watering Hanging Baskets and Window Boxes
These need plenty of water in summer. All you need is a suitable watering can and a tap. The customer provides a stool or step ladder.

52. Dead Heading
Most plants do better when someone picks off the dead flowers. No equipment - just neat fingers and a basket to put the dead heads in. Put them on the compost heap afterwards.

53. Carting Manure

Manure helps plants to grow. It is usually available free from farms and riding stables. A fork or spade, a barrow and your oldest clothes, and you're in business. Dig in a little at the foot of each rose bush.
WARNING - fresh manure "burns" plants and also contains harmful weed seeds; ask for well-rotted manure.

54. Shovelling Snow

After a heavy snowfall, anyone with a snow shovel is in demand. Clear driveways and dig out snowbound cars! Work from one side to another, clearing a path between two snowbanks. NEVER leave a pile of snow at the bottom of anyone's driveway - how will they get their car over it?

CARETAKING

People need someone to take care of things when they go away on holiday.

55. Watering Gardens
Remember to water early in the morning or in the evening, not under full sun.

56. Watering House Plants
Get detailed instructions: you can kill plants with kindness as well as with neglect!

58. Caring for Fish
Goldfish in garden ponds need to be fed. Ask for a packet of fish food and follow the instructions. Which leads us to...

57. Checking Letter boxes
Thieves love empty houses, and newspaper and letters in the letter box are a dead giveaway. Push letters and newspapers right inside.

ANIMAL MAGIC

There is money in pet care. Many people are glad of someone to feed their cats or walk their dogs. Here are some jobs you could do.

59 - 63. Minding Small Pets
(there are so many things you can do here, we've counted them as five ideas!) Rabbits, guinea pigs, mice, gerbils, fish, terrapins, canaries, budgies, lizards, stick insects - all need looking after while their owners are busy or on holiday. You could do this by taking them into your own home (ASK PERMISSION!), or by checking on them twice a day in their own place.

This is not a job you can neglect. Pets are living things which will die if they are not properly looked after. Make sure you know exactly what each creature needs, and give it without fail. How would YOU like to be left all day in a dirty cage with no food or water?

64. Caring for Cats

Offer to feed cats, wash and refill their water bowls and maybe empty their litter trays while owners are on holiday. Give each cat plenty of love and attention as well as food. Always tell a grown-up if a cat seems ill or off its food.

65. Walking Dogs

Many people have to go out to work, leaving their dogs at home all day. Also, many old people cannot exercise their dogs. If you love dogs, walking them is the job for you. Always get to know the dog before taking it out on your own. Never let a dog off the lead where it could cause trouble - near traffic or where small children are playing. Friends can exercise several dogs at the same time and everyone has lots of fun.

66. Grooming Dogs

If you have a way with dogs, you can offer a grooming service for animals you know and trust.

> **You need:**
> Bristle brush for hairy breeds
> Comb
> Wire brush for woolly breeds
> Old rug for the dog to stand on
> Check chain and lead to hold the dog

You may like to work in pairs, one holding the dog and telling it how wonderful it is, the other grooming. Be firm, but gentle. Pay special attention to ears (tell the owner if the ears look red or sore in any way) and feet (check for thorns and burrs). NEVER try to groom a dog you do not know well.

67. Training Dogs

If you are good with dogs, you could offer to train them for other people. Teach them to walk nicely on a lead, to come, sit, fetch, down and stay. Don't expect instant success every time - some dogs, like some people, are slow learners.

68. Mucking out Horses and Ponies

Horses and ponies in stables need feeding, watering and mucking out. This is not a way to get rich quick, but some riding schools will pay you in riding lessons.

69. Caring for Horses and Ponies Outdoors

Someone may pay you to keep an eye on a horse or pony, fetching fresh water and checking the animal is OK.

70. Caring for Chickens

Feeding chickens, cleaning out the nest boxes and collecting the eggs is a popular job for country children. Sometimes they are paid in eggs - well, eggs are very saleable. And gardeners will sometimes pay for a load of well-rotted chicken manure.

71. Scooping the Poop

Not a pleasant job, but someone may pay you to shovel away horse droppings from a paddock or dog dirt from a garden. Wash your hands afterwards! It need not be a messy job. Use a shovel and wear plastic gloves.

72. Pets for Sale

If your guinea pigs, rabbits, gerbils or even stick insects have babies, you could advertise the babies for sale when they are old enough to leave their mothers. It is vital, however, to make sure they go to kind and caring homes. If possible, inspect the animal's future living quarters. You could also provide instructions on caring for it.

SELLING YOUR SKILLS

73. Reading
Many people, while not actually blind, cannot see well enough to read. You could read newspapers, letters, etc. for someone like this. You could also earn money by...

Reading to small children
- especially if you are a fluent reader with the ability to do "funny voices"!

75. Hearing Children Read
Many parents seem to be too busy to hear their little ones read. You could do this on a regular basis. Be kind and patient - everyone has to learn.

76. Helping with Homework
Testing spellings, tables, etc. But NOT actually doing it for them!

77. Teaching Music
Most children want to learn an instrument. It could be a recorder, a violin even a trumpet. Unmusical parents may like to pay a musical genius to teach the child where to put their fingers and how to blow/scrape in the right places. Also to read music and to understand the rudiments of theory.

IF YOU HAVE THE KNACK . . .

78. Teaching Computing
A young friend of mine has been programming computers since he was six years old and has taught many parents and children how to use their new machines. He did it for free. Someone might pay you.

79. Setting Videos
A technophobe is someone who cannot operate a video recorder and is proud of it. You could set their videos for them, to enable them to record the big movie instead of the second half of the News and the first half of their least favourite soap opera.

80. Setting Timers
Modern houses are full of gadgets - ovens, central heating boilers, etc. - with clocks on them, which need resetting after every power cut. You could be the local expert who goes around resetting these gizmos.

81. Typing
Many young people type better than their elders. If you are one of them, you can offer a typing service.

82. Sewing on Name Tapes
Schoolchildren need name tapes on all their gear. If you are nifty with a needle, you can earn money by sewing them on. All you need, apart from the tapes themselves, is a needle, a reel of cotton and a pair of scissors.

83. Sewing on Buttons
As above. Save the buttons from a few old garments to replace lost buttons.

CARING FOR OTHERS

If taking care of children or sick or elderly people appeals to you, you can earn some money and help people at the same time. In an ideal world we'd all do such things for love, but the people we do them for often feel happier if they actually give something in return. A girl I know minded small children and sat with sick people from an early age. She is now a senior nurse in a big teaching hospital.

84. Babysitting
Under-14s should "sit" only for people they know well, and should always be within easy reach of a responsible grown-up. You might babysit for a neighbour, for example, provided you could telephone them (or your own family) in an emergency.

85. Minding Small Children
You could take babies and toddlers to feed the ducks, escort small children to and from playgrounds and so on.

86. Taking Children to and from School
Working mums will often pay a sensible older child to walk their children safely to and from school.

87. Sitting with Old, Sick or Disabled People

Carers who look after someone old, sick or disabled are often glad of someone to "hold the fort" for a short time while they go shopping, etc. And it's nice for those same old, sick or disabled people to have someone young and cheerful around. You may find yourself threading needles for an old lady who loves sewing, but can no longer see to thread her needles; or tying shoelaces for someone who is too stiff to reach them. Perhaps you will feed a disabled child while his Mum gets on with something else. All this is valuable experience if you are considering a career in medicine or social work.

88. Waiting for the Gas Man

Not as dramatic as caring for the sick, but just as important is sitting in, waiting for the gas or repairman/parcel post while someone goes out to work. You can get on with your own work while you're waiting, and save someone from having to take a day off work.

ARTS AND CRAFTS

Making things to sell is very satisfying. There are craft fairs all over the country. Why not ask someone who regularly takes a stall at such fairs to take you and your wares along? Here are a few ideas for money-making "make-its".

89. Selling Plant Cuttings

Some plants, such as geraniums and fuchsias, are ridiculously easy to take cuttings from. And yet plants are quite expensive to buy.

> **You need:**
> A sharp knife
> Some potting compos
> Some little pots (eg. yogurt pots with holes pierced in the bottom)
> An old pencil

Using the knife, take cuttings from the parent plant (see picture). Trim each cutting, as shown. Put some compost in each pot, and water it well. Poke a hole in the compost with the pencil and pop a cutting in. Keep your cuttings warm and watered.

90. Growing Baby Trees

Acorns, horse chestnuts are easy to grow into baby trees. Soak them well before planting. Great oaks from little acorns grow, but so do tiny Japanese "bonsai" trees - the choice is yours!

91. Growing Bulbs
Garden bulbs such as muscaria (grape hyacinth) multiply and have to be thinned out. Take the extra ones, grow them in yogurt pots and sell them when they are sprouting nicely.

92. Selling Garden Produce
Some green-fingered children have gardens of their own and sell their produce. There is always a market for good lettuces and radishes, for example, or bunches of fresh herbs.

93. Selling Flowers
If your flowers have done well, why not make posies to sell? Small flowers like polyanthus make the best posies. Arrange with a few leaves, and tie with knitting wool. If you have plenty of lavender, dry it in bunches to sell.

94. Making Homemade Sweets

Homemade sweets, in pretty boxes (save likely-looking boxes and cover with pretty paper), are very saleable. Here are two recipes which need no cooking.

Peppermint Creams

> **You need:**
> 500g icing sugar • 1 egg white • 1 tsp. lemon juice • Peppermint essence • drop of green colouring • Paper sweet cases

Wash your hands! Then mix everything in a bowl to a stiff paste. Sprinkle icing sugar on the kitchen worktop and roll out the mixture to 1 cm thick. Cut out little rounds with a pastry cutter or bottle top and put each round in a paper case. Put to set in the fridge.

95. Chocolate Truffles

> **You need:**
> 100g cooking chocolate • 100g cake crumbs • a little jam • cocoa powder • paper sweet cases

Melt the chocolate in the microwave or in a bowl over a pan of hot water. Then mix in the cake crumbs and jam. While the mixture is cooling, put a little cocoa powder in a saucer. Wash your hands. Make little balls and roll in cocoa powder. Put each ball in a paper case and leave to set in the fridge.

96. Gift Tags

You need:
Old birthday and Christmas cards
Pinking shears or sharp scissors
Compasses
Pencil
Ruler
Glue
Something to punch holes with
Ribbon, string or knitting wool
Old newspaper to protect your work surface
Small plastic bags

Choose attractive motifs from the old cards, including messages, and cut them out carefully (pinking shears give lovely crinkly edges).

Now cut squares, circles, etc. out of the blank parts of the cards, using your ruler and/or compasses when necessary.

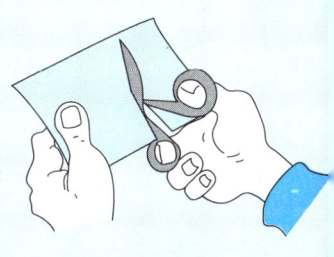

Stick pictures and messages on your gift tags.

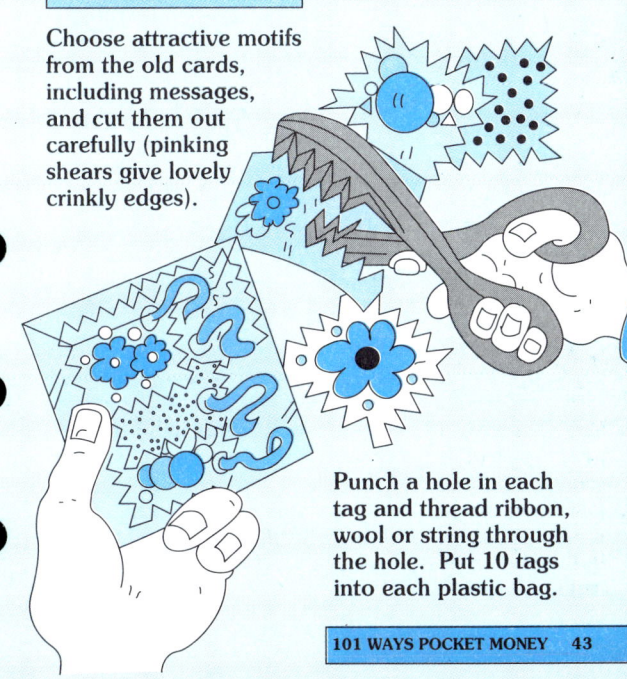

Punch a hole in each tag and thread ribbon, wool or string through the hole. Put 10 tags into each plastic bag.

97. Lavender Bags

A lavender bag hanging in the wardrobe or linen cupboard makes everything smell sweet. They are quite easy to make.

You need:
Dried lavender flowers (no stalks)
Thin fabric (polycotton is ideal; so is net)
Pinking shears or scissors
Needle and cotton
Ribbon

98. Lavender Dolls

You need:
Old-fashioned "dolly" pegs
Lavender
Fabric
Ribbon
Pinking shears
Needle and cotton

Cut a circle of fabric for the skirt. Fill the centre with lavender and lie the peg head inside. Tightly wrap cotton or ribbon around the neck.

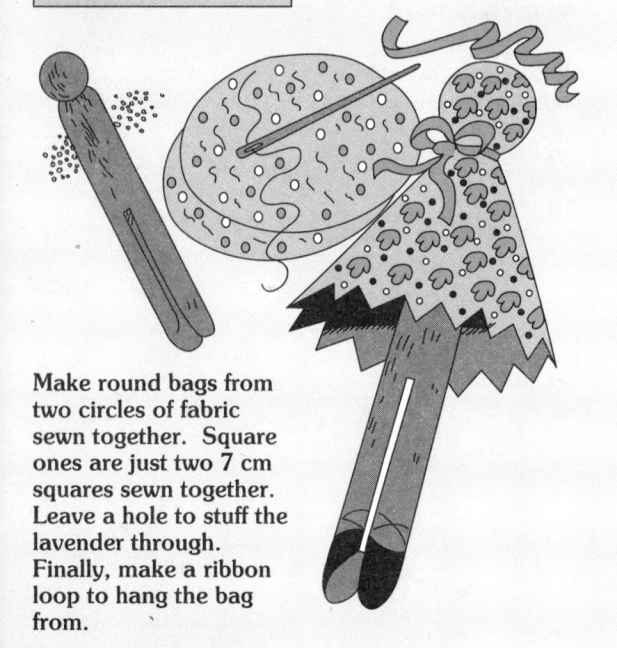

Make round bags from two circles of fabric sewn together. Square ones are just two 7 cm squares sewn together. Leave a hole to stuff the lavender through. Finally, make a ribbon loop to hang the bag from.

PRETTY PRESENTS

The best presents are made from things which would otherwise be thrown away. This set of drawers will look super on anyone's desk (holding paperclips) or dressing table (for earrings).

99. Mini Chest of Drawers

You need:
6 empty matchboxes
Glue
Pretty wrapping paper or wallpaper
Scissors
6 paper fasteners

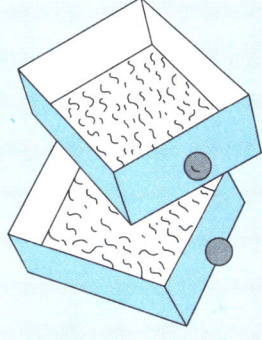

Put pretty paper in the bottom of each drawer.

Glue the matchboxes in three layers of two.

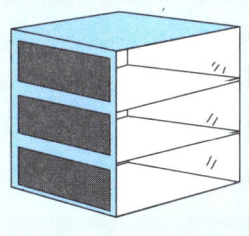

Carefully cover the box part with paper and glue firmly. Put the drawers back.

Take the drawers out of the boxes, and fit a paper fastener in each one for a drawer handle.

100. Beautiful Notebooks

Simple bookbinding can transform a boring note pad or notebook into something to be proud of.

You need:
Stiff cardboard • metal ruler • craft knife • scissors • fabric (for the book spine) • pretty wrapping paper or wallpaper • wallpaper paste or diluted PVA glue

Measure the book, and cut two pieces of cardboard half a centimetre bigger all round.

Cut a strip of fabric 4 cm wide and 2 cm longer than the cardboard.

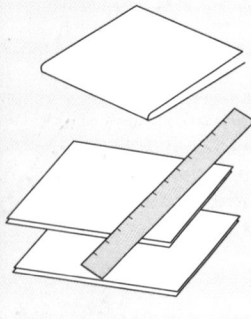

Measure the thickness of the book (call it X), and lay the two pieces of cardboard on the fabric X+ half a centimetre apart.

Stick cardboard and fabric together, and fold over the extra bits of fabric.

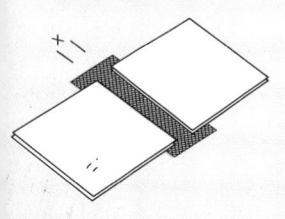

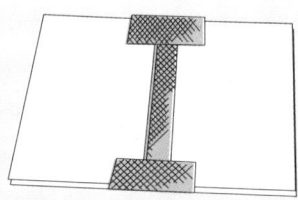

Now, with a craft knife (BE CAREFUL - those things are SHARP!), cut two pieces of paper 2 cm bigger than the book, and stick them to the cardboard, leaving some of the fabric showing.

Make sure there is a good straight edge, well stuck down, next to the fabric spine. Turn in the spare paper, stick firmly. Take your book and fit inside the cardboard folder you have just made. Now stick the first and the last pages to the cardboard. You have just bound a book!

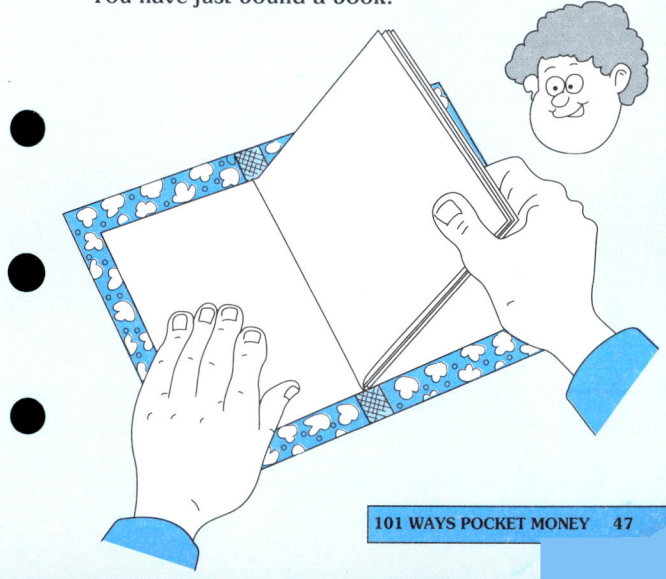

GROWING MONEY

There are many more ways of earning pocket money. You could produce a show and charge admission. Or organise an exhibition of pictures or photos. Plan a pet show, with entrance fees and homemade rosettes. Hold a garage sale to get rid of some of your outgrown clothes and/or toys. Ask permission first.

101. Make your Money Grow
Once you have actually earned some money, you can make it grow by putting it into a savings account. Many banks offer freebies to children who open accounts. Find out what's on offer and decide which of these gifts you would like to own. A money box? A piggy bank? A sports bag? Remember, accounts like these pay very little interest (the money the bank pays you for letting it use your money). You may do better with an ordinary, grown-up building society account. Ask around and find who is offering the best deal.